MARTHA'S VINEYARD WIDE

Early morning in Oak Bluffs Harbor with the distinctive and historic Wesley Hotel in the background.

The Panoramas of A. P. Richmond

Schiffer Publishing Ltd

4880 Lower Valley Road Atglen, Pennsylvania 19310

Dedication

This book is dedicated to Ava Elizabeth and the twins, Charlotte Rose and Charles Douglas.

Schiffer Books are available at special discounts for bulk purchases for sales promotions or premiums. Special editions, including personalized covers, corporate imprints, and excerpts can be created in large quantities for special needs. For more information contact the publisher:

Published by Schiffer Publishing Ltd.
4880 Lower Valley Road
Atglen, PA 19310
Phone: (610) 593-1777; Fax: (610) 593-2002
E-mail: Info@schifferbooks.com

For the largest selection of fine reference books on this and related subjects, please visit our web site at **www.schifferbooks.com**
We are always looking for people to write books on new and related subjects. If you have an idea for a book please contact us at the above address.

This book may be purchased from the publisher.
Include $5.00 for shipping.
Please try your bookstore first.
You may write for a free catalog.

In Europe, Schiffer books are distributed by
Bushwood Books
6 Marksbury Ave.
Kew Gardens
Surrey TW9 4JF England
Phone: 44 (0) 20 8392 8585; Fax: 44 (0) 20 8392 9876
E-mail: info@bushwoodbooks.co.uk
Website: www.bushwoodbooks.co.uk

Contents

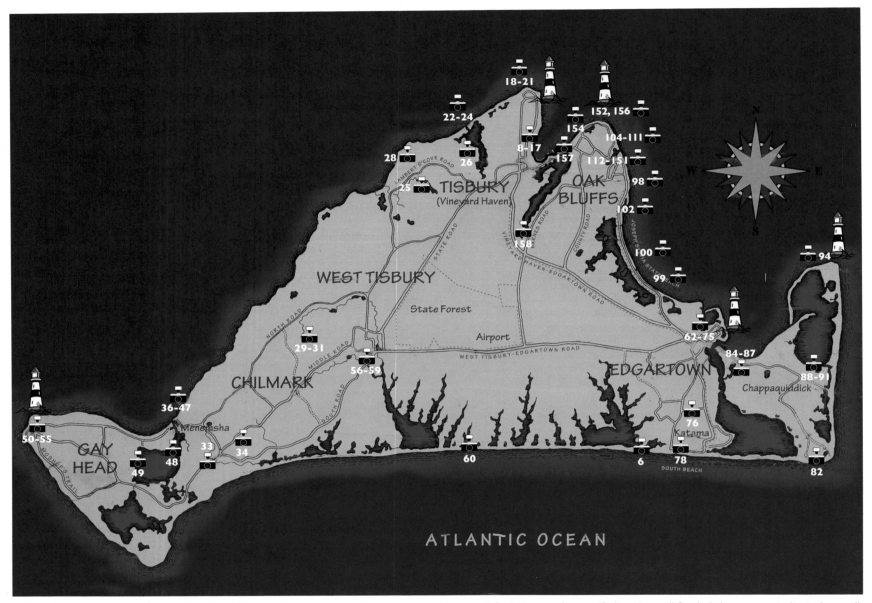

Follow along as we make a loop of the island. The numbers correspond to the pages where you'll find photos of a specific location. All five lighthouses are indicated, as well.

Acknowledgments

It hardly seems possible that this is the fifth book in the *Wide* series. This would not have been possible without the support and encouragement of the editors and personnel at Schiffer Publishing. Thank you to all the guides and local residents who suggested many of the sites found in this book. To Tony Pane, who continues to assist with the English language. To Carol, whose continued guidance has made this possible.

Author's Notes

This is the fifth *Wide* book in a series that includes Cape Cod, North Shore, South Shore, and Boston. As each book has been published, improvements have been made, including a table of contents, an index, and a map that indicates where the images were shot. Readers are able to follow along from page to page as if they were touring the area, or select a specific town or site and proceed directly to that page. In addition, aerial photographs have been taken that give the individual a different perspective of familiar locations.

Martha's Vineyard's island geography has made the images in this book relatively easy to organize, beginning at the ferry dock in Vineyard Haven and making a counter-clockwise loop, passing through the towns of Tisbury, West Tisbury, Chilmark, Aquinnah, Edgartown, and Oak Bluffs, before returning to the starting point. On an island it is possible to capture images that not only reflect the character of each community, but also the charm of Martha's Vineyard itself. This book captures many of the favorite vistas on the island, as well as hidden treasures found off the beaten path. I hope the reader will get as much enjoyment from this book as I have had in shooting these images.

Introduction

Welcome to Martha's Vineyard. Now, follow along with these images as we take a tour of the island that is the destination and summer playground of visitors, artists, writers, celebrities, and U.S. Presidents. Just five miles offshore from Cape Cod, approximately ninety-five square miles in area, and about twenty miles in length, Martha's Vineyard is only accessible by boat or plane. The six towns on the island have a year-round population of about 15,000 people. In the summer, the population explodes, as visitors are attracted by the miles of beaches, the pristine natural locales, the excellent climate that rarely exceeds ninety degrees, and a list of world-class activities.

Although it may have been visited by Vikings more than a thousand years ago, the island was discovered and named by Bartholomew Gosnold, who sailed and explored the coast of New England in 1602. Gosnold is recognized for naming Cape Cod for the abundance of fish he observed in the Provincetown area. New lands were usually named for royalty, but Gosnold, in memory of his daughter who died in infancy, identified the island as Martha's Vineyard. Perhaps without coincidence, it should also be mentioned that Gosnold's mother-in-law, who financed his trip to the New World, was also named Martha. First settled in the mid 1600s, this island has had a storied and historic past. In the nineteenth century, whaling made the island prominent. The name, Martha's Vineyard has remained, and is one of only a few geographical locations in the United States with a possessive place name.

Our journey, which begins in Vineyard Haven, in the town of Tisbury, makes a loop of the island, first heading "up island" to the southwest cliffs of Gay Head, then east to Edgartown and Chappaquiddick Island. We then head northwest towards the cottages and campground in Oak Bluffs before making our way back to our starting point. An island map, which identifies the location of each image, permits the reader to follow along on the journey or to travel to a specific locale. Aerial images are included which offer an additional and different perspective.

Vineyard Haven Harbor is the busiest on the island and most visitors and commercial traffic arrive here from Woods Hole. Yet for all this activity, classic ships and waterfront parks offer the visitor and residents quiet and peaceful spaces. Beyond the harbor, charming shops await the shopper, and magnificent homes of a bygone era are found on the tree-lined streets. At the end of Main Street is the West Chop Lighthouse that guides mariners

into the harbor. Head south out of town and take a right on Lambert's Cove Road and pass fields, ponds, and forests that offer serene and tranquil settings. Some of the sanctuaries along this coast have been preserved for future generations. The next two towns, West Tisbury and Chilmark, are truly rural, with farms and fields of grazing cattle. Less traveled, North Road and Middle Road offer views of tranquility. Chilmark may be best known for its quaint and picturesque harbor, Menemsha. A favorite spot for painters and photographers, Menemsha Harbor also offers shoppers a wide variety of fresh seafood. Just down the road is Aquinnah, formerly known as Gay Head, with its distinctive clay cliffs and the historic lighthouse. It is also the smallest town on the island both in size and population. Private beaches are found along the southern shore.

Heading east, our journey leads towards Edgartown, the largest town both in size and population. Occupying the southeast corner of the island, Edgartown, with its stately homes and churches is reminiscent of its whaling heritage. A grass-stripped airfield and a lighthouse on the harbor are just two of the many attractions in the Edgartown surroundings. Chappaquiddick Island, with its wildlife sanctuary and lighthouse offers visitors to the island a different perspective of Martha's Vineyard. We now head towards Oak Bluffs, probably the most active and lively town on the island. Every morning during the summer season, day-trippers arrive on one of several ferries from the mainland and rent bikes, mopeds, or cars, to tour the island. Some spend the day in Oak Bluffs and step back more than 130 years in time, as they wander past the Victorian cottages of the Campmeeting Association, take a ride on the Flying Horses Carousel, or stroll Circuit Avenue and Ocean Park. In addition, beaches and the harbor offer additional opportunities for various activities. Our tour almost complete, we head towards Eastville and East Chop lighthouse before taking Beach Road past Lagoon Pond and back to Vineyard Haven.

The beauty in this book that travels across the island of Martha's Vineyard is not only the marvelous and splendid panoramas, but in the realization that what you see on these pages is what you would see if you were there. Enjoy and experience scenes familiar to you or explore the vistas that I have captured for the first time.

A gazebo near the ferry dock, overlooking Vineyard Haven Harbor.

A welcome sign greets visitors at the ferry dock.

With excellent roads and an extensive bike trail, visitors can rent mopeds and bicycles. Automobiles and four-wheel drive vehicles are also available.

A variety of classic sailing craft are moored in Vineyard Haven Harbor.

A sailboat heels in Vineyard Haven Harbor.

Just west of the Vineyard Haven ferry docks, these three images are of Owen Park, an idyllic, sandy beach and playground. (Above and following two pages)

World renowned, the ubiquitous Black Dog Tavern became the first year-round restaurant on Martha's Vineyard in 1971. The franchise has expanded to include a bakery, numerous stores, and an unmistakable line of clothing.

Unique shops in downtown Vineyard Haven offer the visitor various and unusual shopping opportunities.

The Nantucket, WLV 612, which was the last lightship in service before it was de-commissioned in 1985.
She has been restored as a luxury yacht with six elegant staterooms and is available for charters.

West Chop Lighthouse is located at the northern tip of land on the west side of Vineyard Haven Harbor. The ferry from Woods Hole that brings visitors to the island passes the lighthouse station with its tower. Two residences and a whistle house (no longer functioning) are in the foreground. Still an active aid to navigation and maintained with Coast Guard personnel, the house on the left is available for rental to service members. The first lighthouse built in this area was originally known as Holme's Hole (1817). The present day tower was built in 1891 and automated in 1976. It now flashes a white signal every four seconds.

19

Looking westerly across Vineyard Sound with the Falmouth and Woods Hole shoreline in the distance.

Beach Plums bloom in the spring along Herring Creek Beach in Tisbury. Locate the cottages and lifeguard stand in the aerial image. The channel leads into Lake Tashmoo. (Above and opposite)

Two views of Lake Tashmoo from Long Beach. This protected area provides access to open waters for a variety of commercial and recreational craft.

Quiet and tranquil, Seth's Pond is an idyllic setting for a young explorer.

Lambert's Cove Road winds through serene and peaceful pastures and provides access to pristine and undisturbed beaches.

Lambert's Cove Road winds through serene and peaceful pastures and provides access to pristine and undisturbed beaches.

Heading "up island," Chilmark offers the visitor rural landscapes with lush and verdant fields. (Above and next page)

Along the back roads, heading "up island" and off the beaten path, remnants of a different era remain.

The farm beyond this stonewall is just a short distance from the center of Chilmark and Beetlebung Corner.

One of Chilmark Cemetery's most famous gravesites belongs to actor John Belushi of *Saturday Night Live*, *Animal House*, and *Blues Brothers* fame.

Here Lies Buried
The Body Of
JOHN BELUSHI

JANUARY 24, 1949
MARCH 5, 1982

I may be gone, but
Rock and Roll lives on.

People relax and enjoy Menemsha Beach on peaceful Vineyard Sound. There is a view of the Elizabeth Islands along the horizon.

A statue of a fisherman spearing a swordfish welcomes visitors
to Menemsha Harbor. The beach is just over the dune.

Using the red roof of the Coast Guard station as a reference, compare this aerial view of Menemsha Harbor with the other two panoramas. (Above right and next page)

Lobsterville Beach and Cranberry Lands, which are just south of Menemsha Creek. (Above and opposite)

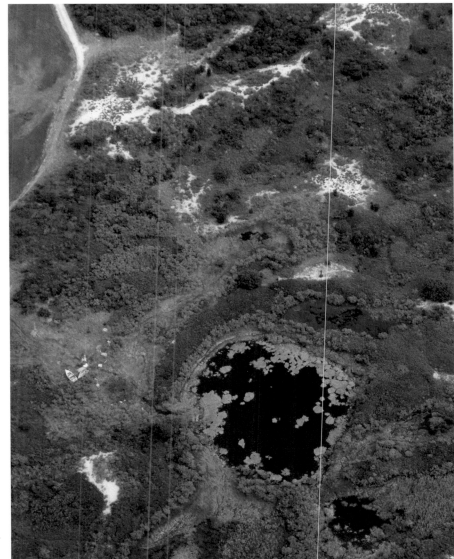

This panorama, taken off-season, shows cottages on Harbor Hill Road overlooking boats docked in Menemsha Harbor.

Left: At the upper end of Menemsha Pond, this boathouse sits on Hariph's Creek. **Right:** On the State Road to Aquinnah, an overlook reveals picturesque views of Menemsha Pond. Menemsha Harbor and the entrance to Vineyard Sound are along the waterway to the right. (Above and opposite)

Near the southwest corner of the island, the red brick Gay Head Lighthouse sits atop the distinctive clay cliffs. To the right are the shops and the overlook that allows visitors to observe the cliffs and lighthouse. The lighthouse, still an active aid to navigation, is maintained by the Martha's Vineyard Historical Society, and is open to the public during the summer season. (Left above and right)

Once a popular tourist destination where visitors could climb the tower, Gay Head Light is all that remains of the keepers' houses and other buildings.

Waves crash along the shore just south of the clay cliffs and Gay Head.

The rural town of West Tisbury extends cross island from the Vineyard Sound shore to the Atlantic Ocean in the south. The center of town is located on the south shore and includes iconic structures such as the white-steepled Congregational Church, the interior of the agricultural hall, the 150-year-old Alley's General Store, and a street named Music because of the number of pianos found in the homes. (Above and opposite)

West Tisbury, with its farms and fields, provides fresh flowers for the passers-by. The weekly farmers' market has a bounty of fresh vegetables, fruits, and flowers. (Above and opposite)

Along South Beach, what was once an opening to a pond, has now filled in with sand. Four-wheel drive vehicles can access this secluded stretch of sand.

A classic flat pergola with benches allows sightseers to spend some time in this quiet park in Edgartown.

Edgartown's South Water Street has numerous Inns. In the background, next to Captain Thomas Milton's house is the Pagoda Tree. Planted in 1837, the captain brought the tree home in a flowerpot from one of his voyages to China. (Above and opposite)

A variety of Greek revival homes face Edgartown Harbor.

In downtown Edgartown, many of the ship captains' homes are hidden by fences and hedges. (Above and opposite)

Edgartown Harbor, which was once the destination of whaling ships, now welcomes large cruising vessels to its safe and protected harbor.

Decorated for the holidays, Edgartown Light with the sun setting across Edgartown Harbor. A single sailboat remains moored in the harbor during the winter season.

Two views from the Edgartown Light—the harbor and town are in the distance. "Red right returning," is a mariner's axiom about the light that flashes red every six seconds and helps to guide mariners into the harbor. The first lighthouse was built here in 1828, when the whaling trade brought vessels into the harbor. Now automated and maintained by the Martha's Vineyard Historical Society (MVHS), the tower is open to the public during the summer season (*courtesy of MVHS*). (Above and opposite)

For more than eighty years, Katama Airfield, with its grassy landing strips, has welcomed planes to its 130 acres between Edgartown and South Beach. Sometimes visitors fly in for a day at the beach, which is just a short walk across the street. Or, visitors can take an aerial tour of the island in the vintage Waco biplanes.

South Beach, just south of Katama Field, is a popular destination for summer visitors.

The free Wi-Fi at the Edgartown Free Public Library attracts off-hours visitors.

The southeast tip of Martha's Vineyard, which is on Chappaquiddick Island, is known as Wasque Point and includes East Beach (seen here). **Left:** Looking west towards Katama Bay there is a recent break in the beach. **Right:** Looking north towards Cape Pogue Wildlife Refuge, Cape Cod is in the distance. (Above and opposite)

With the Edgartown Lighthouse in the background, decorative tents are part of the Chappaquiddick Beach Club.

Preserved areas on Chappaquiddick Island includes this grassy woodland
and a shoreline view of Brine's Pond. (Above and opposite)

At the end of Dike Bridge Road, this wood-beamed overpass leads to the Cape Pogue Wildlife Refuge. Compare the aerial image seen here to the panorama on this page and to the two wide-angle views on the next page. (Left and opposite)

Small boats and kayaks are common craft near the dike bridge. (Above and opposite)

There are several Indian burial grounds on Martha's Vineyard.
This one is situated on North Neck on Chappaquiddick Island,
overlooking Cape Pogue Bay.

Cape Pogue Lighthouse, located at the northeast tip of Martha's Vineyard. (Above and opposite)

Felix Neck Wildlife Sanctuary is one of the most pristine areas on the island.

A nice summer day packs the beaches on Nantucket Sound from Edgartown to Oak Bluffs. (Above and opposite)

This bridge along Beach Road was made famous in the movie *Jaws*.

These golfers are playing the fourteenth hole of the Farm Neck Golf Course. Sengekontacket Pond is in the distance.

Rock jetties mark the entrance to Oak Bluffs Harbor. Beaches stretch along the shoreline. (Above and opposite)

People enjoying the summer weather on a beach in Oak Bluffs.

This hotel in downtown Oak Bluffs is decorated for the Fourth of July.

Two views of Oak Bluffs Harbor: one from the balcony of the Attleboro House and the second at sunrise looking toward Vineyard Highlands.

Built in 1859, the spiritual and cultural center of the Campmeeting Association is this unique iron Tabernacle. Seen here in winter, the Tabernacle, which is listed on the National Register of Historic Places, provides a venue for graduations, summer church services, lectures, and concerts. The distinctive interior is exceptional in American architecture. Designed and built by John W. Hoyt, he also donated the stained glass found over the entrance. (Above and following page)

A must-see when visiting the campground, the Cottage Museum features the interior furnishings of a typical cottage during the late-1800s. This interior view is of the living room, which was used when entertaining guests.

Built closer together, the cottages created a friendly atmosphere. Residents greet passing visitors from the rockers on these porches. (Above and next page)

Many of the cottages, used only in the summer, are still furnished as they were more than 120 years ago. This living room and bedroom are typical of many of the well-maintained cottages. (Above and opposite)

Throughout the campground, which was laid out more than 140 years ago, clusters of cottages are found in distinct parks. A sidewalk runs down the middle of Cottage Park (Top). Forest Park is a circle of about a dozen cottages. (Bottom)

Walking through the campground, each cottage is more unique and exceptional than its neighbor. This is just four of more than 300 cottages that were built in the mid- to late-1800s. (Left and next two pages)

On the third Wednesday in August, Grand Illumination Night celebrates the end of another summer season. The cottages are decorated with Japanese and Chinese lanterns, and after dark, at a designated signal, all the lanterns are lit. Other festivities include a band concert and a community sing-a-long. (Above and next page)

Ocean Park in Oak Bluffs, where the cottages are larger and newer than those in the Campground. (Above and next page)

The Gazebo in Ocean Park during winter (Top) and summer (Bottom). Compare these two images to the previous two panoramas of Ocean Park and identify the various cottages.

Circuit Avenue in Oak Bluffs was named for the ministers that used the street to circle the Campground. The distinctive Victorian Arcade, built in the late 1800s, once housed the post office and the local administration. (Left and next two pages)

The Flying Horses Carousel, originally built in Coney Island, New York, in 1876, was brought to Oak Bluffs in 1884. Listed as a National Historic Landmark, the carousel is the oldest operating platform in America. The horse's tails and manes are not only original, but made of actual horse hair. (Above and next two pages)

The Union Chapel was built in 1870 as a non-sectarian house of worship, and as an alternative to the Tabernacle in the Campground. Octagonal in shape, the chapel has excellent acoustics, which make it a popular setting for concerts, lectures, and weddings. It can hold nearly 400 people. (Above, right, and next two pages)

144

More than 100 years apart, these two images of the Wesley Hotel are a familiar site to boaters in Oak Bluffs Harbor. The last of the grand hotels, the Wesley has been welcoming visitors since 1879. (Above and opposite)

Water views in Oak Bluffs are common. **Left:** Boats moored in the harbor. **Right:** Sunset Pond with the highlands in the background. (Above and opposite)

On Vineyard Sound, the Woods Hole-Oak Bluffs ferry dock is located on Seaview Street. This dock has welcomed visitors to Oak Bluffs for more than 100 years. (Above and opposite)

As early as 1828, signals were sent from Telegraph Hill to mark the passing of ships through Vineyard Sound. Seen here, the cast iron East Chop Lighthouse was built on Telegraph Hill in 1875. Now automated, the tower is maintained by the Martha's Vineyard Historical Society and is open to the public during the summer season. The green light flashes every three seconds, followed by three seconds of dark (*courtesy of MVHS*).

This aerial view shows cottages lining the shore in East Villa

Nearly eighty feet above the water, East Chop Light guides mariners between Oak Bluffs Harbor to the east and Vineyard Haven Harbor to the west. Visitors to the lighthouse park are afforded views of passing ships in Vineyard Sound with the coast of Cape Cod in the distance.

Top: With the bridge raised, a sailboat enters Lagoon Pond. **Right:** An aerial image of the same Lagoon Bridge on Beach Road, which links Oak Bluffs (to the right) with Vineyard Haven (to the left). Lagoon Pond is in the foreground with Vineyard Haven Harbor in the distance. Eastville Point Beach is on the right side of the image, just beyond the bridge.

Quiet and serene, these boats are moored at the upper end of Lagoon Pond.

Bibliography

Burroughs, Polly. *Guide to Martha's Vineyard*, Tenth Edition. (Old Saybrook, CT: The Globe Pequot Press, 2004).

Dennis, Lisl and Burroughs, Polly. *Martha's Vineyard, Houses and Gardens*. (Boston, MA: Little, Brown and Company, 1992).

Hidden Boston and Cape Cod. (Berkeley, CA: Ulysses Press, 2006).

The Island of Martha's Vineyard: 2009 Visitors Guide. (Vineyard Haven, MA: Martha's Vineyard Chamber of Commerce, Inc., 2009).

Weintraub, David. *Walking the Cape and the Islands.*(Birmingham, AL: Menasha Ridge Press, 2006).

Additional resources include: brochures, pamphlets, guides, magazines, volunteers, docents, and interpreters at various island sites.

Index